What people are saying about

Word of the Day

Marilyn Horowitz and her *Word of the Day: Transform Your Writing in 15 Minutes a Day* method have an intensity, brilliance, and originality that are disarming and delightful. They seed the conditions for trust, creativity, and great finished work to emerge. When Marilyn tells you you're a writer, do your voice and the world a favor. Believe her.
Lisa S., Writer

Rather than bringing yet another set of theoretical tools to the table, she leads the student to the living tools already within us.
Brad W., Writer

I'm very grateful to be able to learn from Marilyn. Her focus on the psychological and spiritual foundations necessary to create was integral to my ability to produce a first draft. The tools and structure she teaches made writing easier than I thought it could be!
Kellen G, Writer

When I was stuck at some plot point, Word of the Day helped me think more freely about other possible paths. For a novice screenwriter like myself, who works alone, this became an invaluable tool. Recently, when I revised my first script so I could write the words THE END with confidence I found that the process helped me like a spiritual muse.
Debra H., Writer

Marilyn is the queen of simplicity. Oh, writing is never simple and life doesn't go on autopilot once you hear her take on it, yet it will be something you won't want to forget or lose. Now that could be said of her classic *4 Magic Questions of Screenwriting*, in WOTD she actually does simplify a process. It's a thinking tool, and I, even as her techniques' most undisciplined user, can testify to getting clues, unraveling deadlocks, and trusting oneself when an idea seems to disconnect.
Sandeep G., Writer

Marilyn seems to understand each of her students' artistic direction and supports them with that knowledge. Her Word of the Day formula for storytelling is effective not only for figuring out one's writing, but for life's direction, too. Thank you. If it hadn't been for Marilyn, I don't think I would have made the Woodstock film which will be at the psychedelic film festival at the Producer's Club in November. I got it done.
Nancy C., Writer

For ten years (!) I was imprisoned with an idea that I had a deep passion for but felled by a lack of confidence and living with a belief that I had no business trying to write a 120-page screenplay. I felt the pain of that thorn in my side every single day...After 10 years of stress it only took me 10 weeks to write. 152 pages! And it's GOOD! I am proud of myself beyond words.
Brian G., Writer

The Word of the Day Practice helps to clarify and distill my thinking; it encourages me to be willing to voice what I really want (e.g., shift items from my "dreams" to my "goals/ objectives"), and it brings up interesting connections I wouldn't have previously considered, necessarily. I entered The Big Apple Film Festival and my screenplay was a quarter finalist. :)
Amy B., Writer

Thanks for your Word of the Day Practice. Don't know why the critic comes into us so much. For me, it's when I'm almost done with a piece (composition). Now I know what it is and how to keep it at bay.

Marlene S., Writer

Working with Marilyn Horowitz has challenged every aspect of my creative process from conception to preparation, and most importantly, execution.

Larry L., Writer

Word of the Day

Transform Your Writing in
15 Minutes a Day

Word of the Day

Transform Your Writing in 15 Minutes a Day

Marilyn Horowitz

with

Elizabeth Wiseman

BOOKS

Winchester, UK
Washington, USA

JOHN HUNT PUBLISHING

First published by O-Books, 2024
O-Books is an imprint of John Hunt Publishing Ltd., 3 East St., Alresford,
Hampshire SO24 9EE, UK
office@jhpbooks.com
www.johnhuntpublishing.com
www.o-books.com

For distributor details and how to order please visit the 'Ordering' section on our website.

ISBN: 978 1 80341 516 1
978 1 80341 540 6 (ebook)

A CIP catalogue record for this book is available from the British Library.

Design: Lapiz Digital Services

UK: Printed and bound by CPI Group (UK) Ltd, Croydon, CR0 4YY
Printed in North America by CPI GPS partners

The author of this book does not dispense medical advice or prescribe the use of any technique as a form of treatment for physical, emotional, or medical problems without the advice of a physician, either directly or indirectly. The intent of the author is only to offer information of a general nature to help you in your quest for emotional and spiritual well-being. In the event you use any of the information in this book for yourself, which is your constitutional right, the author and the publisher assume no responsibility for your actions.

We operate a distinctive and ethical publishing philosophy in all areas of our business, from our global network of authors to production and worldwide distribution.

Also by Marilyn Horowitz

The Book of Zev
ISBN-10: 1940192781

How to Write a Screenplay in 10 Weeks
ISBN-10: 1466317515

The 4 Magic Questions of Screenwriting
ISBN-10 1466315695

Sell Your Screenplay in 30 Days: Using New Media by Marilyn
Horowitz and Paula Landry
ISBN-10: 1542904625

How to Write a Screenplay Using the Horowitz System:
The High School Edition
ISBN-10: 0979908922

How to Write a Screenplay Using the Horowitz System:
The Middle School Edition
ISBN-10: 0979908930

"There is only one corner of the universe you can be certain of improving, and that's your own self."

Aldous Huxley

Contents

Acknowledgements

My deepest thanks: I couldn't have done it without you!

Nathan Brandon
Jafe Campbell
Neil Fiore
Lester Hoffman
Paula Landry
Adam Nadler
Beth Ann Price
Gabrielle Rico
Martin Sherlock
Elizabeth Wiseman
My Wonderful Students
The Creator of All Things
Those Who Watch Over Me

Introduction

The Word of the Day Practice is a fifteen-minute daily journaling process that will permanently upgrade your writing. By writing as soon as you wake up and learning to manage your time differently, the whole experience of your writing life can become more joyous and productive. My goal in this book is to help you create at will, write as much as you want, and acquire self-acceptance. To achieve this, I ask you to share this inner adventure and commit to thirty days of doing the **Practice**.

After twenty-five years of teaching writers, I've concluded that success doesn't come merely from perseverance or talent. The degree to which you accept yourself as a writer is the extent to which your *readers and viewers* will accept your work. From this moment on, please ignore the myth of the tortured artist and instead take on the belief that freely doing what you were meant to be doing—that is, writing—is what will make you happiest. Writing will lead you to accept yourself for who you are, and that is the truest form of success. The commercial presentation of a writing project and its path in the marketplace must be separated from its creation.

While intention is crucial to the success of every journey, whether literal or metaphoric, without trusting your decisions until you reach your destination, be it a rewrite or a word change, you will not reach the goal. Belief plus self-respect equals self-acceptance, and this is the antidote for writing pain and procrastination. Most suffering comes from over-identification with your writing process and harsh self-judgment on the quality of the work. Guiding you to transform your writing relationship with yourself from self-critical to self-accepting is the purpose of this book.

The goal of any life should be self-acceptance. It's hard to dive without a diving board and accepting that you are fine just the way you are will set your creativity free, and become the springboard of your success. But creativity must have an outlet, so writers must write. Writing leads to objectivity about what you're writing, and the **Word of the Day Practice** will help you to uncouple your feelings of self-worth from your productivity as a writer. Don't confuse the work with your self-worth. This isn't easy, but by remembering that you exist as a person, separate from your work, you will free yourself from these old chains. Once you can see what is actually going on with your writing, you can objectively assess each situation. If you keep track of how much time you spend writing, you will know whether it's enough for you to accomplish your goals. Decision equals choice, and choice is freedom. But time isn't the only challenge we face.

Many potentially great stories are never finished or completed because our fears of rejection and humiliation are so great it's hard to get past them. This terror feeds our self-doubt, which leads to self-criticism. This makes you afraid to truly write what you mean, so the pages you produce between the margins of fear aren't up to your own standards. You may not even generate a high enough page count. You also probably don't have enough time in your day to write. So you begin, run out of time, doubt yourself, and self-criticize. This is like going on a road trip from home to a weekend getaway. You start with good intentions, but as you drive, self-doubt kicks in, so you hesitate mid-journey and return home. Once home, you reconsider, then start again, but you never arrive at the intended destination. Writing without time management can be a lot like this failed road trip. Worst of all, you've done it to yourself. Your own indecisive behavior drives you to doubt yourself, and the whole fruitless cycle begins again.

One of my students worked on a story about the writer wife of a famous author. After five years and seven drafts, Shari came to me for help. Each draft was like the aforementioned doomed journey. She got halfway through a draft, then the story dwindled and petered out. What became clear was that Shari over-identified with her main character, who had not succeeded, so she was angry at her own creation! Once she was willing to see why her character had failed, she found compassion for the writer wife, and reconnected to her. Her scene work came to life! Next, we focused on Shari's fury at her own lack of success, using the **Word of the Day Practice** to explore her personal writing issues; she was also the wife of a well-known writer! After thirty days, we were able to reorganize her various drafts into a compelling screenplay. The **Practice** allowed Shari to create the same degree of acceptance for herself as she had for the character in her story. She has continued the **Practice** and recently sold a new script.

Let me ask you a question: "Are you crazy?"

If you think that doing the same thing over and over and expecting a different result is sane, I invite you to reconsider. This is a fantasy, just like the idea that we can change anything that has already happened, so don't dignify it! Whenever you feel doubtful of your abilities, reject the thought outright and remind yourself about the good things you already did that day. If you want to improve, you must behave differently, because what you do is who you are. Good behavior creates self-approval. Self-approval releases the fear of failure and rejection. And once you stop doing this *to yourself*, the world will stop "doing" it *to you*.

The world reflects back to you whatever you believe about yourself. We hold onto old behavior and beliefs because our practical selves use patterns from the past to assess the present and predict the future. While they help us survive, these patterns don't allow "presentness," that is, being in the moment, which is the key to original thinking. Patterns can only be changed by becoming aware of an old habit and exchanging it for a new one. The first step is to use the tools here to see where you are functioning on automatic pilot. Notice how you talk to yourself. Notice what you do during a writing session. Do you fidget or answer email? Self-awareness will show you where the old pathway is, then you can choose to walk another one. Once you recognize a pattern, you can interrupt and change it through persistent repetition.

Use the Word of the Day Practice to Build a New Habit

To succeed, you must identify and replace the bad habit with a good habit, and self-doubt is nothing more than a bad habit! Remember when we were told it was okay to smoke cigarettes? How did that turn out? The suggestion that questioning and doubting ourselves is good for us is like saying smoking won't give us cancer. A bald lie! Self-doubt is also an addiction and must be treated as such. When I replaced self-doubt with self-awareness, by using an early version of the **Practice**, I was able to stop smoking in thirty days because I replaced the habit of smoking with a new habit: to chew gum whenever I wanted to smoke. After a few more months, I'd stopped chewing gum.

As an aside, the relationship between writing and life can be described as a dance of metaphor and action, an alchemical relationship whereby an outer action or event can be interpreted on the level of metaphor. In the film *The Wizard of Oz*, Dorothy's discovery that she could have returned home anytime because she wore the ruby slippers is an example of the elegance of metaphor. The red shoes are a symbol of the dormant power within each of us. The ability to extract metaphor from external events is one of the hallmarks of great writing, so use the **Word of the Day Practice** to strengthen your metaphor muscles.

Why We Don't Choose Self-Acceptance

Using the **Word of the Day**, I explored why I would choose to be self-critical instead of self-accepting, and the answer was clear: I wasn't choosing. I was walking down an old road that seemed better because it was familiar. But I'd confused familiarity with safety. Smoking was never safe and could have led me to a painful old age riddled with disease. My behavior at that moment defied logic; how could I believe that any self-destructive relationship could be better than a good one? It was the same when I explored how I treated my creative-writer self. If I imagined myself as a separate person whom I was in a writing partnership with, I would never choose someone who would beat me up for the smallest infraction! When I talked to myself, I sounded like my old geometry teacher shouting at me in my seventh-grade class. "You're stupid, and you'll always be stupid," instead of a supportive colleague giving a thumbs-up and saying with a smile, "C'mon, you can do it. You've done it before and you'll do it again. I believe in you."

Like most people, I'd been brainwashed into thinking that criticism was a more powerful motivator than encouragement! From the moment I began writing in school, my work was graded and critiqued for what was wrong, rarely for what was original. As a trusting child, I accepted my teachers' judgment, not just that my writing wasn't good but that I *myself* was somehow wrong and, therefore, needed to be fixed. So I accepted being corrected harshly by my parents, teachers, and other mentors. Most of them didn't know any better, because they'd been educated in the same destructive manner, and thus believed that using negativity was the proper way to teach.

We all know what a hope-crushing and painful experience being harshly criticized is. That's why we protect ourselves with a layer of insulation by doing it to ourselves first. This reaction comes from the universal fantasy that says by taking often inappropriate responsibility, we can gain power over a situation. If we criticize ourselves first, then we have control. If others condemn us without our agreement, then we feel powerless.

How to Win

Fight back and get off the hamster wheel by eliminating the habits of self-doubt and self-criticism by replacing them with **Accurate Self-Encouragement**. Praise yourself for any writing you do, and remind yourself that all good writing is rewriting, but that you need something to revise. This doesn't mean overlooking mistakes; it means seeing mistakes for what they are, part of a process, not a confirmation that you are doing or being something wrong. Any writing is good writing.

If you can separate measuring your self-worth from completing the task at hand, your productivity will skyrocket. Writing as soon as you wake up will help you make this important distinction. We writers desperately need to *be writing* in order to feel okay. It's who we are. And who we are is not simple.

Writers Are Complex Beings

For the purpose of powerfully transforming ourselves in thirty days, please accept this simplified view of our consciousness. Our identity has two components: our practical everyday self and our imaginative creative self. We need both selves to survive in the same way we need both sides of our brain to work together.

The practical self is created from our biological identity. We rely on this self to navigate the ordinary parts of our lives. This self is our personality, the face we show to the world. This is what we "wear" as we live our daily lives. It's the part of ourselves that gets things done. On the other hand, our creative self is where our imagination lives. It's the unique and original part of ourselves that was often shamed and humiliated for being itself and has been hiding to avoid more criticism and pain. Our creative self is gentle, pure, and lives only in the moment, so, like a stray cat or dog, it must be slowly wooed to trust us and show itself again.

Also remember that our practical self is *not* the enemy, like, say, my geometry teacher, as is so often suggested when referred to as the "inner critic." Instead, think of it as a protective parent who doesn't want their child to be hurt! However, since we are no longer kids, we must find the courage to defy that controlling parental inner voice and risk writing what we mean. By being able to instantly merge the two aspects of yourself, you can create a supportive, unconditionally loving relationship with yourself so that, every time you write, you will be inspired by the full force of your imagination. Wow! The **Word of the Day Practice** will give you the confidence to write authentically, one word at a time.

After a week or so of consistently performing the entire **Word of the Day Practice**, your viewpoint will shift, because the primary source of doubt has been removed. You will no longer be oppressed by the concern about whether or not you are writing, because you just wrote! By the end of the thirty days, you'll find that your attention has become focused on the writing itself rather than on your writing performance—the key to **Accurate Self-Encouragement**.

Overview

The **Word of the Day Practice** is easy and fun. You'll start your day by finding a **Word of the Day** and growing it into a **Word of the Day cluster**. Then, by comparing your original word and a contrasting word, you'll easily create a story idea, and write it out in a sentence or two as if it were a description on a TV channel menu.

Much of our emotional turmoil comes from the past. Our creative mind doesn't understand time, which is one of the reasons structuring a story is so hard. This lack of understanding is also part of the reason that we are haunted by things that have already—or never—happened. The creative mind doesn't understand the concept of "it's over" or "before"; it only understands "now." You can see why what you do in the present moment defines how you feel about yourself. To correct this problem, you'll create a quick list of your writing intentions, such as "work on my story an hour a day," and a quick list of your beliefs about writing, such as "I will complete this script in ten weeks." Next, you'll incorporate these two lists into an imaginary writing schedule as if you were looking back on the day that's passed. These two steps will take you ten minutes or less.

At the end of your day, right before bedtime, you'll put in just five more minutes, writing about how your day actually went, and then comparing it with your **Ideal Day**. Without judgment or any pressure to actually change anything, you can enjoy the possibility that you can create the writing life you want.

The **Word of the Day Practice** is the fastest route to **Accurate Self-Encouragement** and, ultimately, self-acceptance as a writer that I have found so far.

Writers hate themselves when they haven't written, and they are often their harshest critics even while writing. The **Word**

of the Day Practice is the preventative to such self-loathing because you write every day, *right away*, starting with just one word, preferably while you're still in bed.

I worked with an actor who was also a stand-up comedian. He'd been very ill and away from his career for several years, but he had been asked by one of the big streaming services to write a comedy show about his illness. He was completely blocked. So, using the **Word of the Day Practice**, he began to write in bed as soon as he woke up in the morning. I also put him on a word "diet." He wasn't allowed to write a single word more than the steps allowed for. The reverse psychology worked, and by the end of the month, he had an outline and comedy bits for his show, which was a big success. He's kept on doing the **Practice** for several years now, and reports that he feels peaceful as long as he does the work.

How to Do the
Word of the Day Practice: Step 1

The best way to succeed at anything is to do what you love first. As soon as you awaken, you can create magic in your writing life by drawing a single word inside a circle. Think of the first word that comes to mind, and if you can't find a word, use the word "writer." That'll get you going! Grab your timer. Please use pen and paper because writing by hand connects you to a different part of your brain than typing does. I want you to access that part when doing the **Practice**.

Preparation

You must prepare for any important task. Professional runners visualize how they will perform, and being relaxed before a race is a necessary component for success. Writing is a physical activity, so let's follow their lead and relax first. This is useful not only before this practice but each time you write, and will help increase your productivity.

Do This Before You Write:

1. Say aloud, "I now intend to work in a state of **Accurate Self-Encouragement**."
2. Smile.
3. Close your eyes, rolling them up toward the space between your eyebrows.
4. Take three slow, deep breaths.
5. Visualize yourself writing "The End" or "Fade Out."
6. Gently open your eyes and grab your pen.

Create Your Word of the Day

Set your timer for one minute. Do the breathing prep and ask for a word to appear in your mind. Some writers see the word as if it were on a movie screen, some hear an inner voice say it, and some writers feel it in their body. You'll know when it's *the* word, because it will reach you separate from any other thought or feeling. I "see" my words on a mental screen between my eyebrows. I have recently gotten the following words: "tea," "butterfly," and "telegraph."

It doesn't matter what the word is. Again, if you can't think of a word, just use the word "writer."

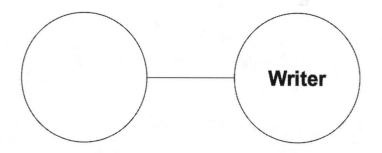

Write your word inside the circle. Congratulate yourself because *"I wrote, therefore I am."*

The next step is to continue by expanding this word into a word cluster. Set the timer for one minute and free-associate about the word until the timer goes off. Here's how to do it:

1. Repeat your intention to use **Accurate Self-Encouragement!**
2. Using the word in the circle on your page, draw another circle nearby and write a word inside that circle.
3. Draw a spoke from your **Word of the Day** circle to the new circle.

4. Create more circles with new words in them and attach your new circles to each other.
5. Fill new circles with words that relate to the other words.
6. Do it until your timer goes off, the page feels full, or you feel done.

Your resulting page may look like a cloud of balloons or may have crazy offshoots in many directions with bubbles extending every which way. The goal is for you to feel happy and optimistic. Don't think too hard or worry, just let the words encourage other words to emerge. The words don't need to "match" or follow any formula; this is the equivalent of a kid with crayons drawing whatever they want. You're *playing with words*, and it should be totally enjoyable!

For example, here's a one-minute cluster based on the **Word of the Day**, "moxie."

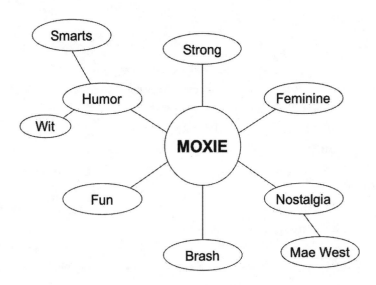

As you can see, "moxie" is the central circled word. Then the brainstormed words go outward around the main word. Write whatever you're thinking and join it to the main word with a line. By connecting the **Word of the Day** circle to other word circles, you create a constellation, and each word relates to the central word like the planets around the sun. You've created a world and have approached "The Final Frontier," your creative mind! Woo-hoo! The goal is to feel happy and optimistic, whatever those words mean to you. The point is not the shape you make, or even the exact words you select, but the pleasure you can have brainstorming.

During this process, a seemingly unthematic word will appear, and you'll feel a shift in your flow. That's when you stop. This is the word we want to find, but without looking for it. There are many paradoxes in the authentic creation process, and this "finding without looking" is one of them. Further, there are no accidents in this process, and this contrasting word is the key that will unlock the door to an original story idea.

The Conflict Word

The **Conflict Word** is like a grain of sand inside an oyster. The friction of the unwelcome granule inside of the shell is how this mollusk makes pearls. Because our conflict word contrasts with our **Word of the Day**, there's disagreement, and a break in our streaming thought. In this interruption is the kernel of a good story. The creative self loves to make connections between disparate ideas. No matter whether the word is an ugly duckling or a swan, this word is a gift. Just as you rub two sticks together to build a fire, rub the **Word of the Day** and the **Conflict Word** together to make creative sparks fly.

The **Conflict Word** in the moxie cluster was "spiderweb." So, where could the contrast between "moxie" and "spiderweb" lead? For Paula, a dear colleague, finding the conflict resulted in a story called "Moxie," about a fearless heroine in a sci-fi story who, on her quest, is trapped in a giant spiderweb—and though she's normally unshakeable, she's terrified of spiders. How she overcomes her fear and escapes will make for fascinating reading and/or viewing.

In my version of the story, a little girl rescues her big sister from an evil spider-witch, who has the world trapped in her web. In rescuing her sister, the little girl breaks the spiderweb and sets the world free. What is *your* version? Write it down in the space provided below:

How fun was that? This is your imagination at work. You took two words and combined them to create something new that has never existed before! Wow! Seeing continuous daily proof that you are a storyteller will build your sense of self-worth with effortless grace and speed.

You may have noticed that my request for your version set off your story-making machine instantly and without self-consciousness. And you may also have immediately squelched the idea that started to bubble up. This is the conflict between your two selves at work: the creative self, who gets inspired and starts to create, and the practical self, that biological-survival machine, who shuts that self down with a disparaging remark. Why does this happen? Because the biological-survival self is afraid of conflict, which it reckons as a source of danger, and fears anything that is not actually happening in the current moment. The biological brain relies on past patterns to assess what is truly happening, and any break in the pattern is perceived as a threat. Now you know why you experience resistance when you're trying to write.

Experiment Now

Take a risk. Draw a circle, think of a word, and put it in the circle and cluster until you think of a word that contrasts with the word you chose. For example, if your word was "writer," your brainstorming words might be "famous," "computer," "thoughtful," or "hardworking," and then the word "ballerina" appears in your mind's eye. What does "ballerina" have to do with "writer"?

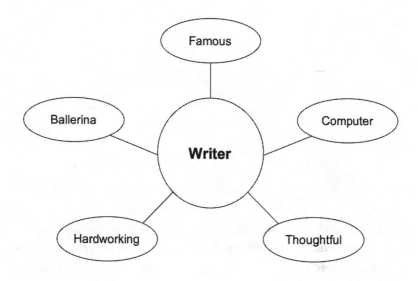

That little tickle of excitement you just felt in your brain—your heart beating a little faster with joy at exploring a possible connection between the two words, and a vague visual image forming somewhere behind your eyebrows—is exactly what the first part of the practice is about! Don't block your imagination; write freely in the space provided below. For example, I might write "How's a ballerina related to a writer? They're both precise, hardworking, and entertaining. A writer is as skilled as a ballerina, but a ballerina is dancing someone else's story and a writer makes up their own."

The last part of the practice would be to write down a one- or two-line story idea for your own **Word of the Day** and **Conflict Word** as you did for the moxie/spiderweb **Word of the Day**. Here's what this exercise suggested to me: A love story about a writer and a ballerina, with the typical genders reversed.

Get excited about your story "kernel" because you've just created something new and unique!

Your Story Idea:

Expanding the Kernel into a Story

Let's use our moxie/spiderweb cluster to develop your concept further. The **Word of the Day cluster** is like a Swiss Army knife with many attachments, so you can use the simple process over and over as you expand your ideas. A **Conflict Word** cluster becomes your starting point.

1. Use your **Word of the Day Conflict Word** to create another cluster, like the one on page 17 (top).
2. Continue brainstorming words as you expand upon the chosen word until you find another word that is opposite, conflicting, or adversarial. In this case, I came up with the word, "flykiller," which is really two words but came up in my mind as one, so I permitted it.
3. Then compare the two words by creating a **Conflict Cluster**, placing them side by side and drawing a circle around both, then clustering around them until you start to get ideas for a story. See the bottom image on page 17 as an example.

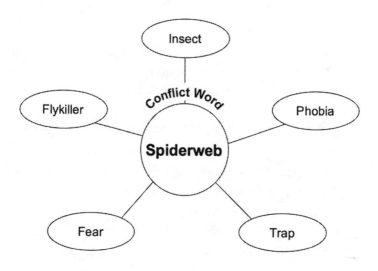

4. To further your process, do some research. In my case, the word seemed tangential, but since I trusted in my ability to make up a story, I got on the internet to find out what and who else kills flies. Were there other "flykillers" in nature? Research showed me something terrific, that

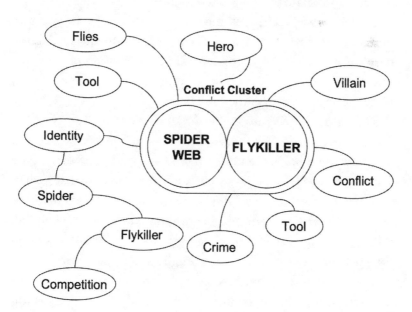

there are "assassin flies," predator flies that eat other flies. That made me wonder what ecological function flies serve besides being spider fodder. Further research revealed that, "while you might find flies maddening, lots of animals you love rely on flies for their food. Birds, lizards and frogs all enjoy chowing down on tasty flies (as does my dog)." So, we know insects already play an essential role in the web of life, but new research shows they could be doing even more. While you might not want them spewing on your snag, they could be the food that fed the pig to make the snag." (I got my inspiration from blog.csiro.au/five-reasons-flies-are-awesome/)

So here was the motherlode of the story: The spider-witch has to be convinced not to eat any more flies, because between her and the assassin flies, the entire ecology of the planet would be destroyed! Suddenly, my little girl became the bullied daughter of the local Australian exterminator. It's her father who's taught her how to stop bugs, which enables the little girl to team up with the witch, who repurposes the web to catch only the assassin flies. The witch is fed, the planet is saved, and the little girl's heroism is acknowledged by her former tormentors. Maybe it's not *War and Peace*, but it's a solid, original story with a layered plot, and most importantly a relatable hero and several villains, including the Witch and the Lord of the Assassin Flies. The little girl's allies include: the Leader of the flies, her dad, a wizard, and an oracle, who helps the little girl see her own importance in the world ecology. The story now has a full cast and a clear story arc.

I sat in wonder as my little **Word of the Day** blossomed into an allegory of the eternal battle of good versus evil, complete with backstory, societal implications, and a subplot! Also, the blog is from Australia, an interesting location for a story.

As a side note: to get further and faster in the development process, start with a location. Like real estate, location in writing is critical. Where your story is set will help you make strong choices and avoid mistakes, because we all know what can or can't happen in a particular place.

A good story uses both imagery and analogy to tell us something about ourselves. It's what's often called "the message" or "the moral." In this case, the moral is that even the lowly fly has an important function in the world. A story becomes compelling because, in the analogy to our theme with the plot, we can find the metaphor of the hero's or heroine's journey. Here, the little girl first sees herself as being as inconsequential and as annoying as a fly, but by the end of the story she cannot fail to acknowledge her own worth.

Name Your Story

Naming your story is like signing a painting. You take ownership over what you've created: an intellectual property that, if developed, could bring the happiness you seek. Your practical self will respond with more support if it sees there's a potential tangible reward for writing, and your creative self likes to name things. While the final title will often be very different than this first attempt, a title helps position the compass that will guide the ship of your story into the right port.

I like to parody the titles of other successful books and movies, so an obvious choice would be to use *The Lord of the Flies* as a jumping-off point and reframe it for my new heroine: *Princess of the Flies*, because she's female, and a little girl.

Conclusion

This first step of the **Word of the Day Practice**, which you have now completed, is a powerful storytelling tool that will lead you to writing self-acceptance. Remember: A story a day keeps writer's block away. Let's move on to Steps 2 and 3 of the **Word of the Day Practice**.

How to Do the Word of the Day Practice: Steps 2 and 3

Your Ideal Day and the Review of the Day

"The easiest thing in the world to do is not to write." **Stephen King**

Now that you understand how to use the **Word of the Day**, let's explore how we can use the next steps of the **Practice** to manage our time in a more satisfying way. All that we really have is our time, and how we spend it today determines our writing futures. That nagging feeling of guilt you sometimes have is a sign that you might not be using the present moment to its fullest.

Steps 2 and 3 of the **Practice** will guide you to a better understanding of what you expect from yourself and what is possible each day. With this information, you can re-adjust your self-expectations to a realistic level of daily writing productivity, which will increase your ability to **Accurately Encourage** yourself.

Writing Success

Observation is a powerful tool when used without the need for an opinion of what's being studied. Every successful writer finds the time to write, so please understand that there is no "magic secret." You must *regularly* put aside the time to write, or you will fail. Daily pre-arranged spaces written into a schedule, and keeping this appointment, guarantee a continuous bridge to permanent self-acceptance. The problem you will encounter is how much time daily life takes up, and how little time is left over to write. We sleep eight hours, work eight hours, and must eat and groom ourselves. The goal of this part of the process is for you to see what you're up against without judgment or pressure. Accepting how little time you really have and allowing the creative self to freely voice its desires will help you organically shift your priorities and get the practical self to cooperate. Even if you write as a job, there are many other demands on your time. I suggest that you begin by looking for fifteen- and thirty-minute spaces in your schedule and plan your writing accordingly. If you commit to a half hour daily, you can get a lot done. An hour is even better, even if it's broken up. Regularity is something the practical self understands. If you are already pretty well organized, finding more pockets of time will only create more opportunities.

Making Peace with the Practical Self

The practical self can be persuaded to cooperate with the creative self by a daily demonstration. It recognizes your priorities and rates them. If the first thing you do when you wake up is to open your eyes, so that the practical self can assess where you are and gauge safety, and the next action is to write, the practical self will connect writing with seeing and include it as a fundamental survival skill. The practical self's purpose is to help you stay alive, and your behavior is demonstrating that writing is part of *your* survival. Since survival is the practical self's imperative, this repeated experience will convince it to stop offering up such powerful resistance. Remember the image of water dripping on stone and wearing it away. The **Practice** is the water, and your resistance is the stone. Keep dripping!

Why Is There So Much Resistance?

The practical self is hardwired for survival. It's the part of you that manages your autonomic nervous system, which is basically a machine in your subconscious that ensures primary functions, such as your breathing and heartbeat. As you may remember, the practical self is just trying to protect you from danger, and views rejection and humiliation as potentially fatal.

When we were infants and children, our survival depended on the goodwill and love of our parents and other caretakers. Were you ever yelled at, hit, or sent to bed without supper? If so, then you know firsthand that the fear of death was a great motivator for you to cooperate with your punishers.

Often our unresolved memories of being censured or ridiculed remain open wounds, and we live in fear of a repetition. We can overcome our terror by giving ourselves **Accurate Self-Encouragement** and finding a way to put the past in the past.

How to Conquer the Past

Consider the old question about a tree falling in the woods. If you don't hear it fall, did it make a noise? Now ask yourself: if I don't think about the past, did it happen? For our purposes in this book, the answers are that the tree didn't make a sound and the past never happened.

Remember that the creative self lives only in the present, and if you remain focused on the here and now, there will be no place for the past in your thoughts. When you're in the moment, the practical self can't cast its web of past patterns over you, giving you an opportunity for transformation.

Change your habits of thought, and you change your life. From this moment forth, approach writing with an attitude of self-acceptance: you will make mistakes, but a mistake can be corrected. Legend has it that the *Mona Lisa*'s smile was an error that da Vinci decided to keep. Mistakes are opportunities to see things freshly. Simply choose to reframe how mistakes actually function in the overall process of success, for without a basis of comparison, how can we improve?

Use a Mantra

The motto of my writing system, which has taught hundreds of first-time writers to complete a readable screenplay in eight weeks, is *Don't Get It Right, Get It Written.* Repeat this phrase often and connect to feeling good about yourself in a relaxed way. Practicing the feeling of self-approval will encourage you to deliberately ignore thinking about the past, so you can create new patterns, which create new habits, which retrain the practical self to participate.

You Must Decide

Life is literally what you make it. We compromise in our relationships because we've been taught that you must give up something to get something, so we turn ourselves into pretzels to get love and approval. This is another lie, because real relationships are about two people sharing a conversation, not one person making themselves less so the other can be more. After many relationships, you may have lost sight of what you want when not considering anything or anyone else. It's critical to recover this knowledge because it will affect the quality of your work.

A Magic Question

To reconnect with yourself, you need to become more aware of what is happening with you on a moment-by-moment basis. The way to clarity is to constantly ask yourself if what you are doing right now is acceptable to you; and if it isn't, then ask yourself what you need to do to make it okay.

Answering this question—and honoring your answers—will wear away all self-doubts, like dripping water wears away stone. The practical self seeks to protect you by blocking your own access to your creative self in any way it can, whether through indecision, jumbled thinking, exhaustion, and, most effectively, self-criticism, which is fed by self-doubt. If you know what is and what isn't acceptable, self-doubt and indecision can no longer exist.

Overcoming the Biological Imperative

This work is serious business, because you're up against a biological imperative that thinks it's helping you to survive by keeping you small. Don't minimize this powerful force or attempt to confront it. Better, do an end run around it and reframe the situation positively by finding a solution that allows you to write more.

For example, whenever you feel that you have "writer's block," just start retyping a favorite piece of *someone else's* writing. Within a page, you will find yourself rewriting and, thus, be inspired to write yourself.

Another idea: when you don't know what to write, go on the Internet and research your general subject until you find something that interests you. When I was developing the story about the spider-witch, I researched spiderwebs. That's when I discovered that there were assassin flies who ate other flies, and that flies are an essential part of our ecological system since they provide food for so many other species.

A last word: judging your writing at this stage is a bad habit. Stop doing it! *Write first, assess later.* Your job is to create, not be the salesman of your project. The quality of the writing is not your job at this juncture. This is why rewriting should be done only AFTER you create a first draft.

How to Create Your Ideal Writing Day Cluster

In the same way we use the **Word of the Day**, the act of clustering about your current writing intentions and beliefs will entice the creative self to voice what is real, distinct from the external demands accepted by the practical self. The key is to work fast and suspend making judgments; your goal is *quantity*, not *quality*. Desire inspires intentions, and intentions inspire action. The more you attune to your desire to write, the more likely it is that you will find enough time to do so.

Writing includes research, journaling, reading, and, yes, watching TV and movies. Be sure to include time for these in your imaginings. Estimate the time required to complete each intention.

My Writing Intentions

1. Draw a circle in the top of your page and write "My Writing Intentions" inside.
2. Set your timer for one minute.
3. Write as fast as you can. You'll average five to eight intentions. Some examples are: "Write for one hour," "Research new story," and "Journal three pages."

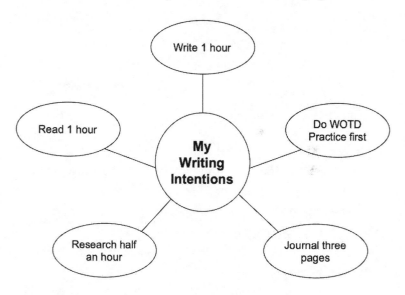

My Writing Beliefs

1. Draw a second circle here and write "My Writing Beliefs" in the center.

2. Again, set the timer for one minute.
3. Quickly list five or more beliefs, such as "I believe I can succeed." Focus on believing, and it will turn into knowing, which will reinforce your intentions regarding writing.

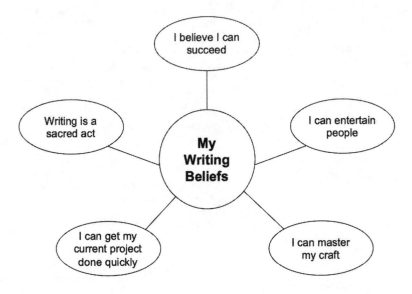

Now create your Ideal Writing Day using the daily planner. Think of it as an anti-planner because you're scheduling your life *before* you fit the writing in. Begin by putting in the other events planned for the day, such as "eat breakfast," "work 9-5," "sleep 8 hours," and so on. Then put your writing sessions in the time left over.

You may be shocked at how little time is left to write. Decide what you can realistically achieve. Every day you will find it easier to fit in more writing, journaling, and reading. For example, my friend Christine never had time to write. She has two kids, a landscaping business, feeds stray cats, and has a sick elderly dog. About a month after she began doing the **Practice**, she noticed that she spent an hour a day watching TV every morning. She now skips it and spends the time writing, much to her delight. I'm sure there are a few spaces in your day where you could find time to write more.

IDEAL WRITING SCHEDULE

DATE:	MON	TUE	WED	THU	FRI	SAT	SUN

TIME	ACTIVITIES
	MORNING
8am–8:30am	Wake up and meditate
8:30am–9am	Word of the Day Practice
9am-10am	Breakfast
10am-11am	Journal 3 pages
11am-12pm	Take a walk
	AFTERNOON
12pm–1pm	Write for 1 hour
1pm–3pm	Lunch with Lisa
3pm–4pm	Research 1 hour
	EVENING
6pm–8pm	Dinner with family
8pm–9pm	Reading
9:30pm–10pm	Word of the Day Practice
10pm	Sleep

You'll notice that you probably couldn't find time for everything. And that's the point, so there's nothing to do but go about your day, making mental notes of what you're doing and how much time each activity takes. Learning to make time estimates is a crucial skill we all need to improve. Accept that you'd like to have more time and move onto living the rest of your actual day.

Now spend a minute or two writing about your experience. I might have written, "Wow. Moxie. Assassin flies. Who knew? I think I can pass up on the news and read a little this morning. I could squeeze ten minutes of writing into my morning break. I feel excited."

Nightly

Before you go to bed, set aside five minutes to complete the practice below. Set your timer for one minute and make a list (or a cluster) of *what actually happened* in your day, and roughly how long each event took. For example, "sleep: 7 hrs; write: 1 hr; eat lunch: 1/2 hour." During the day, you may not want to jot down each activity, but keep track of how much time you actually spent on writing and related activities.

Nightly Review

CLUSTER

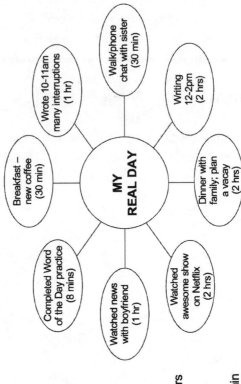

MY REAL DAY

- Breakfast – new coffee (30 min)
- Wrote 10-11am many interruptions (1 hr)
- Walk/phone chat with sister (30 min)
- Writing 12-2pm (2 hrs)
- Dinner with family; plan a vacay (2 hrs)
- Watched awesome show on Netflix (2 hrs)
- Watched news with boyfriend (1 hr)
- Completed Word of the Day practice (8 mins)

LIST

- Word of the Day Practice – 5 min
- Breakfast – new coffee – 30 min
- Wrote 10–11am, with many interruptions
- Walk/phone chat with sister – 30 min
- Wrote 12–2pm, happy
- Dinner with family; plan a vacay – 2 hrs
- Watched awesome show on Netflix – 2.5 hrs
- Watched the news with boyfriend – 1 hr
- Completed Word of the Day Practice – 8 min
- Slept – 8 hrs

Next, you would transfer the listings to your Nightly Review planner as per the sample below.

NIGHTLY REVIEW

DATE:	MON TUE WED THU FRI SAT SUN
TIME	**ACTIVITIES**
	MORNING
9am–10am	Wake up + breakfast (new coffee)
10am–11am	Writing with many interruptions
11am–11:45am	Walk + phone chat with sis
	AFTERNOON
12pm–2pm	Writing
2pm–3pm	Meeting for Work
3pm–5pm	Work, emails, etc.
5pm–5:20pm	Brief revision and project
	EVENING
6pm–8pm	Dinner with family – planned vacay
8:30pm–10:30pm	Watched awesome show on Netflix
10:30pm–11:30pm	Watched news with BF
11:30pm–11:45pm	Completed Word of the Day, Daily review, Planner
11:45pm	Sleep

Now, compare your morning list with what has actually occurred during your day, as listed in your Nightly Review.

Comparing my ideal writing day and my actual writing day

IDEAL WRITING SCHEDULE

DATE:

TIME	ACTIVITIES	MON	TUE	WED	THU	FRI	SAT	SUN
	MORNING							
8am–8:30am	Wake up and meditate							
8:30am–9am	Word of the Day Practice							
9am–10am	Breakfast							
10am–11am	Journal 3 pages							
11am–12pm	Take a walk							
	AFTERNOON							
12pm–1pm	Write for 1 hour							
1pm–3pm	Lunch with Lisa							
3pm–4pm	Research 1 hour							
	EVENING							
6pm–8pm	Dinner with family							
8pm–9pm	Reading							
9:30pm–10pm	Word of the Day Practice							
10pm	Sleep							

NIGHTLY REVIEW

DATE:

TIME	ACTIVITIES	MON	TUE	WED	THU	FRI	SAT	SUN
	MORNING							
9am–10am	Wake up + breakfast (new coffee)							
10am–11am	Writing with many interruptions							
11am–11:45am	Walk + phone chat with sis							
	AFTERNOON							
12pm–2pm	Writing							
2pm–3pm	Meeting for Work							
3pm–5pm	Work, emails, etc.							
5pm–5:20pm	Brief revision and project							
	EVENING							
6pm–8pm	Dinner with family – planned vacay							
8:30pm–10:30pm	Watched awesome show on Netflix							
10:30pm–11:30pm	Watched news with BF							
11:30pm–11:45pm	Completed Word of the Day, Daily review, Planner							
11:45pm	Sleep							

Use the Facts to Make Positive Changes

Comparison is priceless. By acknowledging the differences between the two "days" *without judging or trying to change anything*, you will be able to make changes that will work! The question we're seeking to answer is: "How can I schedule enough time to write?" By seeing how little time we really have, you'll be inspired to both schedule your writing time and to use it. Writing time must become sacred. Writers can no more survive without writing than everyone else can without sleep. Make appointments with yourself to write, and keep them, but forgive yourself if you fail, and use **Accurate Self-Encouragement** to see what happened.

For example, if I wanted to understand how I ended up watching the news instead of meditating, I would recall that my boyfriend had come home late and suggested watching the news together. I hadn't seen him all day and relished the chance to reconnect. Then I would consider whether I'd made the right choice, and was there an alternative?

This is the kind of **Accurate Self-Encouragement** that will help you transform the way you spend your time, because the problem to overcome is now concrete. No one can do two things at once. I suppose I could have tried to meditate while watching the news, but that would have defeated *both* the intention to spend time with my beau as well as the intention to meditate! Not a big deal, but what if the situation had been one where I'd planned to write?

This is where the plot thickens, as it were. If I had scheduled time to write and something else came up, where was my integrity? I would have betrayed myself in order to honor his request, and not even thought about it. Then later, I could criticize myself for some petty infringement instead of dealing with the real issue: I'd betrayed myself and my stated intention to write.

Once you understand how you actually spend your time in ways that don't serve you, the Practice can provide an inner structure to your life and bring about transformation. Use the journal pages provided to explore this and reflect on your day.

Congratulations! You've now completed the entire daily practice. Now draw a circle on a page in your notebook ready for tomorrow.

Conclusion

I have been guilty of reading books about how to improve, thinking that reading about a topic was a substitute for doing the work. It's not. Use the included journal pages and checklist to chart your journey to a more satisfying writing life.

The **Word of the Day Practice** will transform your life if you consistently devote fifteen minutes daily and complete all the steps. Imagine yourself a month from tomorrow morning. You will have created thirty story kernels. You will have made painless and organic changes in your writing life. Most importantly, you will have consistently written something original and addressed your own uniqueness by honoring your intentions and beliefs.

I have many students who have written readable, well-structured screenplays in eight weeks using my writing method. They're always amazed by their achievement, but I remind them that all they did was to get out of the creative self's way. I have no doubt about your talents, so please let me prove to you how unique and dedicated you are by inspiring you to follow this simple regimen.

Here's to your successful writing.

Marilyn

What People Are Saying About the Word of the Day Practice

LIZ: One day my worlds collided. I had a part-time job in real estate, and my goal for this job was to increase the rankings of the various agents. It's really difficult and tedious and takes a while. And I wrote in my beliefs cluster I was going to get someone's ranking up to the highest level that day, which wasn't on the radar at all. And it happened. It was miraculous and shocking.

I started the Word of the Day a little bit later. It wasn't a full two weeks, but things started to just dovetail and streamlined to where I wanted them. You see the before and after, like where things went off and even sometimes the pitfalls you just can't really avoid. So, you have to know to work around it. But definitely the scripted day started becoming closer and closer to reality, in baby steps.

PAULA: This has been fun for me because I wake up with words, then they bounce around in my head all day. I'm working on story and character even when I think I'm not, so the flow has been easier. This practice has led to me knocking out writing right away. Some days I rush a little, but it's so interesting to see where the cluster leads and what a ball it is. I'm really enjoying it! I look forward to seeing where I'm at in two weeks.

BETH: Feeling uneasy and anxious about world events has been affecting my work and personal life. One morning, I picked up my journal and the Word of the Day I chose was UNCERTAINTY. From this word flowed all kinds of negative words. But toward the end, my mindset began to change. Out of anxiety, anger, and frustration, new thoughts emerged, including new ideas; I learned to move out of my comfort zone, innovation, and opportunity.

Now I am finding new ways to organize my time, increase my productivity, and focus more outward and not inward—and all from finding that the emotions and challenges from uncertainty can be channeled into positive action and growth.

MARLENE: Thanks for your Word of the Day Practice. Don't know why the critic comes into us so much. For me, it's when I'm almost done with a piece (composition). Now I know what it is and how to keep it at bay.

SANDEEP: Marilyn is the queen of simplicity. Oh, writing is never simple, and life doesn't go on autopilot once you hear her take on it, yet it will be something you won't want to forget or lose. Now that could be said of her classic "4 Magic Questions of Screenwriting," in WOTD she actually does simplify a process. It's a thinking tool, and I, even as her techniques' most undisciplined user, can testify to getting clues, unraveling deadlocks, and trusting oneself when an idea seems to disconnect.

ALEX: When I began using the word-a-day clustering process, I didn't know where it would lead me. Perhaps it would open some creative portal in my brain that I hadn't been able to access before. Soon I realized that word clustering could be used purposefully. When I was stuck at some plot point, clustering helped me think more freely about other possible paths. When I needed to understand the complexities of a character, clustering helped me understand what belonged and didn't belong to that character.

For a novice screenwriter like myself, who works alone, not in a formal writers' room, word clustering became an invaluable tool. Recently, when I revised my first script so I could write the words THE END with confidence, I found that the clustering process helped me like a spiritual muse. And when I was finally done with that script, the clustering process didn't clamor for attention. I understood that this spiritual muse is resting until I'm ready to call on it again.

About the Authors

Marilyn Horowitz is an award-winning author, New York University professor, TV show creator, and writing coach, working with successful novelists, produced screenwriters, and award-winning filmmakers. Two of her mentees have been nominated for an Emmy®, and a third won a Peabody. Horowitz received the New York University Award for Teaching Excellence in 2004 and has an active online audience comprising 5,000 Facebook friends, over 5,000 connections on LinkedIn, and 1,500 readers of her weekly blog. Since 1998 she has taught hundreds of aspiring writers to complete their feature-length screenplays, novels, and TV pilots using her trademarked writing method, The Horowitz System®. Horowitz has also written five books on screenwriting, two of which are used as textbooks at New York University. In 2022, she was an associate producer of *Hunter Is F**cked*, an award-winning comedy short based on the life of gonzo journalist Hunter S. Thompson. Earlier this year, Horowitz served as a judge for the Big Apple Film Festival in the narrative-feature-film category. In conjunction with the PANO Network, she is currently sponsoring a contest for the best original screenplay. She is passionate about helping aspiring creatives launch their writing careers, and since 2021 has been holding webinars to share her unique creativity-and-time-management technique, *The Word of the Day Practice*. For fiction, she's represented by the Blue Ridge Literary Agency, and her first novel, *The Book of Zev*, was published by Kohler Books. Horowitz is a board member and co-hosts a writer's group for the Florence Belsky Foundation.

Elizabeth Wiseman is a writer/producer, Senior Curator for The Marilyn Horowitz / PANO Screenwriting Award, and a finalist in the Nicholl Fellowships in Screenwriting. She's currently completing a TV pilot, and producing a new short film, *More Than Words*.

Blank Clusters

Word of the Day Cluster

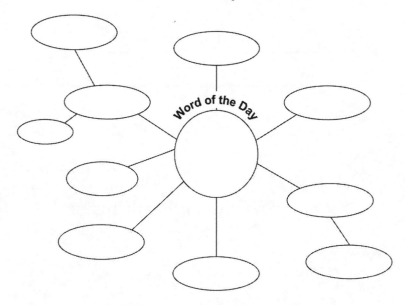

Conflict Word Cluster

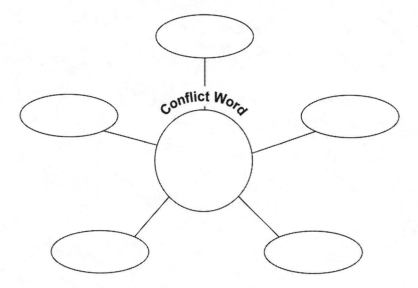

My Story:

My Writing Intentions Cluster

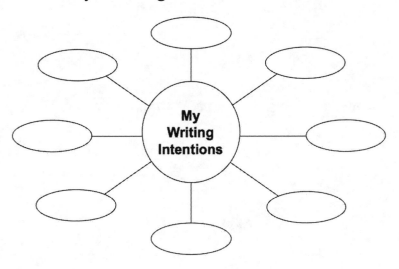

My Writing Beliefs Cluster

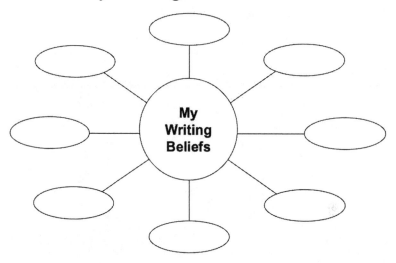

My Ideal Writing Day

IDEAL WRITING SCHEDULE

DATE: MON   TUE   WED   THU   FRI   SAT   SUN

TIME	ACTIVITIES
	MORNING
	AFTERNOON
	EVENING

NIGHTLY REVIEW

DATE:

		MON	TUE	WED	THU	FRI	SAT	SUN

TIME	ACTIVITIES
	MORNING
	AFTERNOON
	EVENING

I'd Like to Change

Word of the Day
30-Day Journal

Put a check in the circle for each day you succeed. Remember, it's better to do a part of the **Practice** than none at all! If you create a **Word of the Day cluster** and don't have the time or energy to do more, give yourself half a checkmark. *Intention equals Success!*

Word of the Day 30-Day Checklist

○ DAY 1	○ DAY 11	○ DAY 21
○ DAY 2	○ DAY 12	○ DAY 22
○ DAY 3	○ DAY 13	○ DAY 23
○ DAY 4	○ DAY 14	○ DAY 24
○ DAY 5	○ DAY 15	○ DAY 25
○ DAY 6	○ DAY 16	○ DAY 26
○ DAY 7	○ DAY 17	○ DAY 27
○ DAY 8	○ DAY 18	○ DAY 28
○ DAY 9	○ DAY 19	○ DAY 29
○ DAY 10	○ DAY 20	○ DAY 30

Journal: Day 1

DATE: _____ PAGE 1

Word of the Day

Word of the Day

Conflict Word

Conflict Word

Conflict Cluster

Conflict Cluster

Story Idea

NOTES

Journal: Day 1

DATE: _____ PAGE 2

Writing Intentions

My Writing Intentions

Writing Beliefs

My Writing Beliefs

Ideal Day Planner

TIME	ACTIVITIES
	MORNING
	AFTERNOON
	EVENING

Word of the Day Diary

Journal: Day 1

DATE: _____ PAGE 3

Nightly Review

TIME	ACTIVITIES
	MORNING
	AFTERNOON
	EVENING

TOTAL HOURS

Writing: _____ Journaling: _____ Research: _____

Ideal Day Planner

TIME	ACTIVITIES
	MORNING
	AFTERNOON
	EVENING

Diary

How would I like to transform my day? How do I feel about my day overall? Did I do enough writing and writing-related tasks?

Journal: Day 2

DATE: _____ PAGE 1

Word of the Day

Conflict Word

Conflict Cluster

Story Idea

NOTES

Journal: Day 2

DATE: _____ PAGE 2

Writing Intentions

My Writing Intentions

Writing Beliefs

My Writing Beliefs

Ideal Day Planner

TIME	ACTIVITIES
	MORNING
	AFTERNOON
	EVENING

Word of the Day Diary

Journal: Day 2

DATE: _____ PAGE 3

Nightly Review

TIME	ACTIVITIES
	MORNING
	AFTERNOON
	EVENING

TOTAL HOURS

Writing: _____ Journaling: _____ Research: _____

Ideal Day Planner

TIME	ACTIVITIES
	MORNING
	AFTERNOON
	EVENING

Diary

How would I like to transform my day? How do I feel about my day overall? Did I do enough writing and writing-related tasks?

Journal: Day 3

DATE: _____ PAGE 1

Word of the Day

Word of the Day

Conflict Word

Conflict Word

Conflict Cluster

Conflict Cluster

Story Idea

NOTES

Journal: Day 3

DATE: _____ PAGE 2

Writing Intentions

My Writing Intentions

Writing Beliefs

My Writing Beliefs

Ideal Day Planner

TIME	ACTIVITIES
	MORNING
	AFTERNOON
	EVENING

Word of the Day Diary

Journal: Day 3

DATE: _____ PAGE 3

Nightly Review

TIME	ACTIVITIES
	MORNING
	AFTERNOON
	EVENING

TOTAL HOURS

Writing: _____ Journaling: _____ Research: _____

Ideal Day Planner

TIME	ACTIVITIES
	MORNING
	AFTERNOON
	EVENING

Diary

How would I like to transform my day? How do I feel about my day overall? Did I do enough writing and writing-related tasks?

_____

_____

_____

_____

_____

_____

Journal: Day 4

DATE: _____ PAGE 1

Word of the Day

Conflict Word

Conflict Cluster

Story Idea

NOTES

Journal: Day 4

DATE: _____ PAGE 2

Writing Intentions

My Writing Intentions

Writing Beliefs

My Writing Beliefs

Ideal Day Planner

TIME	ACTIVITIES
	MORNING
	AFTERNOON
	EVENING

Word of the Day Diary

Journal: Day 4

DATE: _____ PAGE 3

Nightly Review

TIME	ACTIVITIES
	MORNING
	AFTERNOON
	EVENING

Writing: _____ Journaling: _____ Research: _____

TOTAL HOURS

Ideal Day Planner

TIME	ACTIVITIES
	MORNING
	AFTERNOON
	EVENING

Diary

How would I like to transform my day? How do I feel about my day overall? Did I do enough writing and writing-related tasks?

Journal: Day 5

DATE: _____ PAGE 1

Word of the Day

Word of the Day

Conflict Word

Conflict Word

Conflict Cluster

Conflict Cluster

Story Idea

NOTES

Journal: Day 5

DATE: _____ PAGE 2

Writing Intentions

My Writing Intentions

Writing Beliefs

My Writing Beliefs

Ideal Day Planner

TIME	ACTIVITIES
	MORNING
	AFTERNOON
	EVENING

Word of the Day Diary

Journal: Day 5

DATE: _____ PAGE 3

Nightly Review

TIME	ACTIVITIES
	MORNING
	AFTERNOON
	EVENING

TOTAL HOURS

Writing: _____ Journaling: _____ Research: _____

Ideal Day Planner

TIME	ACTIVITIES
	MORNING
	AFTERNOON
	EVENING

Diary

How would I like to transform my day? How do I feel about my day overall? Did I do enough writing and writing-related tasks?

Journal: Day 6

DATE: _____ PAGE 1

Word of the Day

Conflict Word

Conflict Cluster

Story Idea

NOTES

Journal: Day 6

DATE: _____ PAGE 2

Writing Intentions

My Writing Intentions

Writing Beliefs

My Writing Beliefs

Ideal Day Planner

TIME	ACTIVITIES
	MORNING
	AFTERNOON
	EVENING

Word of the Day Diary

Journal: Day 6

DATE: _____ PAGE 3

Nightly Review

TIME	ACTIVITIES
	MORNING
	AFTERNOON
	EVENING

TOTAL HOURS

Writing: _____ Journaling: _____ Research: _____

Ideal Day Planner

TIME	ACTIVITIES
	MORNING
	AFTERNOON
	EVENING

Diary

How would I like to transform my day? How do I feel about my day overall? Did I do enough writing and writing-related tasks?

Journal: Day 7

DATE: _____ PAGE 1

Word of the Day

Conflict Word

Conflict Cluster

Story Idea

NOTES

Journal: Day 7

DATE: _____ PAGE 2

Writing Intentions

My
Writing
Intentions

Writing Beliefs

My
Writing
Beliefs

Ideal Day Planner

TIME	ACTIVITIES
	MORNING
	AFTERNOON
	EVENING

Word of the Day Diary

Journal: Day 7

DATE: _____ PAGE 3

Nightly Review

TIME	ACTIVITIES
	MORNING
	AFTERNOON
	EVENING

TOTAL HOURS

Writing: _____ Journaling: _____ Research: _____

Ideal Day Planner

TIME	ACTIVITIES
	MORNING
	AFTERNOON
	EVENING

Diary

How would I like to transform my day? How do I feel about my day overall? Did I do enough writing and writing-related tasks?

_____

_____

_____

_____

_____

Journal: Day 8

DATE: _____ PAGE 1

Word of the Day

Word of the Day

Conflict Word

Conflict Word

Conflict Cluster

Conflict Cluster

Story Idea

NOTES

Journal: Day 8

DATE: _____ PAGE 2

Writing Intentions

My Writing Intentions

Writing Beliefs

My Writing Beliefs

Ideal Day Planner

TIME	ACTIVITIES
	MORNING
	AFTERNOON
	EVENING

Word of the Day Diary

Journal: Day 8

DATE: _____ PAGE 3

Ideal Day Planner

TIME	ACTIVITIES
	MORNING
	AFTERNOON
	EVENING

Nightly Review

TIME	ACTIVITIES
	MORNING
	AFTERNOON
	EVENING

Writing: _____ Journaling: _____ Research: _____

TOTAL HOURS

Diary

How would I like to transform my day? How do I feel about my day overall? Did I do enough writing and writing-related tasks?

Journal: Day 9

DATE: _____ PAGE 1

Word of the Day

Word of the Day

Conflict Word

Conflict Word

Conflict Cluster

Conflict Cluster

Story Idea

NOTES

Journal: Day 9

DATE: _____ PAGE 2

Writing Intentions

My Writing Intentions

Writing Beliefs

My Writing Beliefs

Ideal Day Planner

TIME	ACTIVITIES
	MORNING
	AFTERNOON
	EVENING

Word of the Day Diary

Journal: Day 9

DATE: _____ PAGE 3

Nightly Review

TIME	ACTIVITIES
	MORNING
	AFTERNOON
	EVENING

TOTAL HOURS

Writing: _____ Journaling: _____ Research: _____

Ideal Day Planner

TIME	ACTIVITIES
	MORNING
	AFTERNOON
	EVENING

Diary

How would I like to transform my day? How do I feel about my day overall? Did I do enough writing and writing-related tasks?

Journal: Day 10

DATE: _____ PAGE 1

Word of the Day

Conflict Word

Conflict Cluster

Story Idea

NOTES

Journal: Day 10

DATE: _____ PAGE 2

Writing Intentions

My Writing Intentions

Writing Beliefs

My Writing Beliefs

Ideal Day Planner

TIME	ACTIVITIES
	MORNING
	AFTERNOON
	EVENING

Word of the Day Diary

Journal: Day 10

DATE: _____ PAGE 3

Nightly Review

TIME	ACTIVITIES
	MORNING
	AFTERNOON
	EVENING

TOTAL HOURS

Writing: _____ Journaling: _____ Research: _____

Ideal Day Planner

TIME	ACTIVITIES
	MORNING
	AFTERNOON
	EVENING

Diary

How would I like to transform my day? How do I feel about my day overall? Did I do enough writing and writing-related tasks?

Journal: Day 11

DATE: _____ PAGE 1

Word of the Day

Conflict Word

Conflict Cluster

Story Idea

NOTES

Journal: Day 11

DATE: _____ PAGE 2

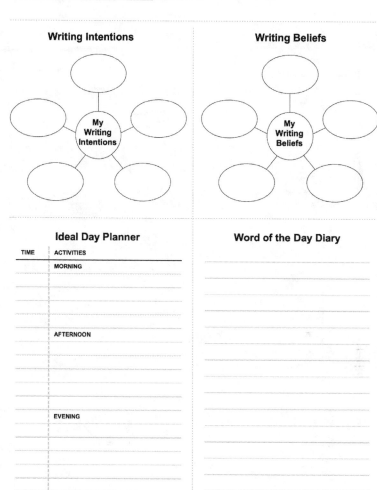

Writing Intentions

My Writing Intentions

Writing Beliefs

My Writing Beliefs

Ideal Day Planner

TIME	ACTIVITIES
	MORNING
	AFTERNOON
	EVENING

Word of the Day Diary

Journal: Day 11

DATE: _____ PAGE 3

Nightly Review

TIME	ACTIVITIES
	MORNING
	AFTERNOON
	EVENING

TOTAL HOURS

Writing: _____ Journaling: _____ Research: _____

Ideal Day Planner

TIME	ACTIVITIES
	MORNING
	AFTERNOON
	EVENING

Diary

How would I like to transform my day? How do I feel about my day overall? Did I do enough writing and writing-related tasks?

Journal: Day 12

DATE: _____ PAGE 1

Word of the Day

Word of the Day

Conflict Word

Conflict Word

Conflict Cluster

Conflict Cluster

Story Idea

NOTES

Journal: Day 12

DATE: _____ PAGE 2

Writing Intentions

My Writing Intentions

Writing Beliefs

My Writing Beliefs

Ideal Day Planner

TIME	ACTIVITIES
	MORNING
	AFTERNOON
	EVENING

Word of the Day Diary

Journal: Day 12

DATE: _____ PAGE 3

Nightly Review

TIME	ACTIVITIES
	MORNING
	AFTERNOON
	EVENING

TOTAL HOURS

Writing: _____ Journaling: _____ Research: _____

Ideal Day Planner

TIME	ACTIVITIES
	MORNING
	AFTERNOON
	EVENING

Diary

How would I like to transform my day? How do I feel about my day overall? Did I do enough writing and writing-related tasks?

Journal: Day 13

DATE: _____ PAGE 1

Word of the Day

Conflict Word

Conflict Cluster

Story Idea

NOTES

Journal: Day 13

DATE: _____ PAGE 2

Writing Intentions

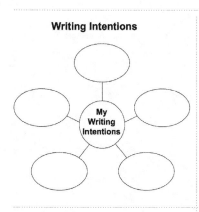

Writing Beliefs

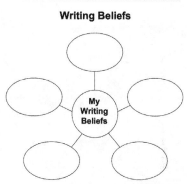

Ideal Day Planner

TIME	ACTIVITIES
	MORNING
	AFTERNOON
	EVENING

Word of the Day Diary

Journal: Day 13

DATE: _____ PAGE 3

Nightly Review

TIME	ACTIVITIES	
	MORNING	
	AFTERNOON	
	EVENING	

TOTAL HOURS

Writing: _____ Journaling: _____ Research: _____

Ideal Day Planner

TIME	ACTIVITIES	
	MORNING	
	AFTERNOON	
	EVENING	

Diary

How would I like to transform my day? How do I feel about my day overall? Did I do enough writing and writing-related tasks?

Journal: Day 14

DATE: _____ PAGE 1

Word of the Day

Conflict Word

Conflict Cluster

Story Idea

NOTES

Journal: Day 14

DATE: _____ PAGE 2

Writing Intentions

My Writing Intentions

Writing Beliefs

My Writing Beliefs

Ideal Day Planner

TIME	ACTIVITIES
	MORNING
	AFTERNOON
	EVENING

Word of the Day Diary

Journal: Day 14

DATE: _____ PAGE 3

Nightly Review

TIME	ACTIVITIES
	MORNING
	AFTERNOON
	EVENING

TOTAL HOURS

Writing: _____ Journaling: _____ Research: _____

Ideal Day Planner

TIME	ACTIVITIES
	MORNING
	AFTERNOON
	EVENING

Diary

How would I like to transform my day? How do I feel about my day overall? Did I do enough writing and writing-related tasks?

Journal: Day 15

DATE: _____ PAGE 1

Word of the Day

Conflict Word

Conflict Cluster

Story Idea

NOTES

Journal: Day 15

DATE: _____ PAGE 2

Writing Intentions

My
Writing
Intentions

Writing Beliefs

My
Writing
Beliefs

Ideal Day Planner

TIME	ACTIVITIES
	MORNING
	AFTERNOON
	EVENING

Word of the Day Diary

Journal: Day 15

DATE: _____ PAGE 3

Ideal Day Planner

TIME	ACTIVITIES
	MORNING
	AFTERNOON
	EVENING

Nightly Review

TIME	ACTIVITIES
	MORNING
	AFTERNOON
	EVENING

TOTAL HOURS

Writing: _____ Journaling: _____ Research: _____

Diary

How would I like to transform my day? How do I feel about my day overall? Did I do enough writing and writing-related tasks?

Journal: Day 16

DATE: _____ PAGE 1

Word of the Day

( )
( ) Word of the Day ( )
( ) ( )

Conflict Word

( )
( ) Conflict Word ( )
( ) ( )

Conflict Cluster

( ) ( ) ( )
( ) Conflict Cluster ( ) ( ) ( )
( ) ( )

Story Idea

_____
_____
_____
_____
_____
_____
_____
_____

NOTES

_____
_____
_____

Journal: Day 16

DATE: _____ PAGE 2

Writing Intentions

My
Writing
Intentions

Writing Beliefs

My
Writing
Beliefs

Ideal Day Planner

TIME	ACTIVITIES
	MORNING
	AFTERNOON
	EVENING

Word of the Day Diary

Journal: Day 16

DATE: _____ PAGE 3

Nightly Review

TIME	ACTIVITIES
	MORNING
	AFTERNOON
	EVENING

TOTAL HOURS

Writing: _____ Journaling: _____ Research: _____

Ideal Day Planner

TIME	ACTIVITIES
	MORNING
	AFTERNOON
	EVENING

Diary

How would I like to transform my day? How do I feel about my day overall? Did I do enough writing and writing-related tasks?

Journal: Day 17

DATE: _____ PAGE 1

Word of the Day

Word of the Day

Conflict Word

Conflict Word

Conflict Cluster

Conflict Cluster

Story Idea

NOTES

Journal: Day 17

DATE: _____ PAGE 2

Writing Intentions

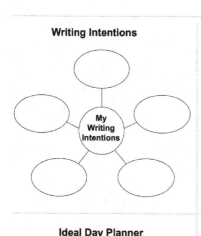

Writing Beliefs

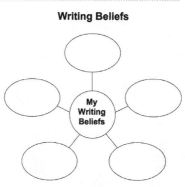

Ideal Day Planner

TIME	ACTIVITIES
	MORNING
	AFTERNOON
	EVENING

Word of the Day Diary

Journal: Day 17

DATE: _____ PAGE 3

Nightly Review

TIME	ACTIVITIES
	MORNING
	AFTERNOON
	EVENING

Writing: _____ Journaling: _____ Research: _____

TOTAL HOURS

Ideal Day Planner

TIME	ACTIVITIES
	MORNING
	AFTERNOON
	EVENING

Diary

How would I like to transform my day? How do I feel about my day overall? Did I do enough writing and writing-related tasks?

Journal: Day 18

DATE: _____ PAGE 1

Word of the Day

(Word of the Day cluster diagram)

Conflict Word

(Conflict Word cluster diagram)

Conflict Cluster

(Conflict Cluster diagram)

Story Idea

_____
_____
_____
_____
_____
_____
_____
_____
_____

NOTES

_____
_____
_____

Journal: Day 18

DATE: _____ PAGE 2

Writing Intentions

My Writing Intentions

Writing Beliefs

My Writing Beliefs

Ideal Day Planner

TIME	ACTIVITIES
	MORNING
	AFTERNOON
	EVENING

Word of the Day Diary

Journal: Day 18

DATE: _____ PAGE 3

Nightly Review

TIME	ACTIVITIES				
	MORNING				
	AFTERNOON				
	EVENING				

Writing: _____ Journaling: _____ Research: _____

TOTAL HOURS

Ideal Day Planner

TIME	ACTIVITIES				
	MORNING				
	AFTERNOON				
	EVENING				

Diary

How would I like to transform my day? How do I feel about my day overall? Did I do enough writing and writing-related tasks?

Journal: Day 19

Word of the Day

Conflict Word

Conflict Cluster

Story Idea

NOTES

Journal: Day 19

DATE: _____ PAGE 2

Writing Intentions

My
Writing
Intentions

Writing Beliefs

My
Writing
Beliefs

Ideal Day Planner

TIME	ACTIVITIES
	MORNING
	AFTERNOON
	EVENING

Word of the Day Diary

Journal: Day 19

DATE: _____ PAGE 3

Nightly Review

TIME	ACTIVITIES
	MORNING
	AFTERNOON
	EVENING

TOTAL HOURS

Writing: _____ Journaling: _____ Research: _____

Ideal Day Planner

TIME	ACTIVITIES
	MORNING
	AFTERNOON
	EVENING

Diary

How would I like to transform my day? How do I feel about my day overall? Did I do enough writing and writing-related tasks?

Journal: Day 20

DATE: _____ PAGE 1

Word of the Day

(Word of the Day cluster diagram)

Conflict Word

(Conflict Word cluster diagram)

Conflict Cluster

(Conflict Cluster diagram)

Story Idea

NOTES

Journal: Day 20

DATE: _____ PAGE 2

Writing Intentions

My Writing Intentions

Writing Beliefs

My Writing Beliefs

Ideal Day Planner

TIME	ACTIVITIES
	MORNING
	AFTERNOON
	EVENING

Word of the Day Diary

Journal: Day 20

DATE: _____ PAGE 3

Nightly Review

TIME	ACTIVITIES
	MORNING
	AFTERNOON
	EVENING

TOTAL HOURS

Writing: _____ Journaling: _____ Research: _____

Ideal Day Planner

TIME	ACTIVITIES
	MORNING
	AFTERNOON
	EVENING

Diary

How would I like to transform my day? How do I feel about my
day overall? Did I do enough writing and writing-related tasks?

Journal: Day 21

DATE: _____ PAGE 1

Word of the Day

Conflict Word

Conflict Cluster

Story Idea

NOTES

Journal: Day 21

DATE: _____ PAGE 2

Writing Intentions

My Writing Intentions

Writing Beliefs

My Writing Beliefs

Ideal Day Planner

TIME	ACTIVITIES
	MORNING
	AFTERNOON
	EVENING

Word of the Day Diary

Journal: Day 21

DATE: _____ PAGE 3

Nightly Review

TIME	ACTIVITIES
	MORNING
	AFTERNOON
	EVENING

TOTAL HOURS

Writing: _____ Journaling: _____ Research: _____

Ideal Day Planner

TIME	ACTIVITIES
	MORNING
	AFTERNOON
	EVENING

Diary

How would I like to transform my day? How do I feel about my day overall? Did I do enough writing and writing-related tasks?

Journal: Day 22

DATE: _____ PAGE 1

Word of the Day

Word of the Day

Conflict Word

Conflict Word

Conflict Cluster

Conflict Cluster

Story Idea

NOTES

Journal: Day 22

DATE: _____ PAGE 2

Writing Intentions

Writing Beliefs

Ideal Day Planner

TIME	ACTIVITIES
	MORNING
	AFTERNOON
	EVENING

Word of the Day Diary

Journal: Day 22

DATE: _____ PAGE 3

Ideal Day Planner

TIME | ACTIVITIES

MORNING

AFTERNOON

EVENING

Nightly Review

TIME | ACTIVITIES

MORNING

AFTERNOON

EVENING

TOTAL HOURS

Writing: _____ Journaling: _____ Research: _____

Diary

How would I like to transform my day? How do I feel about my day overall? Did I do enough writing and writing-related tasks?

Journal: Day 23

DATE: _____ PAGE 1

Word of the Day

Conflict Word

Conflict Cluster

Story Idea

NOTES

Journal: Day 23

DATE: _____ PAGE 2

Writing Intentions

My Writing Intentions

Writing Beliefs

My Writing Beliefs

Ideal Day Planner

TIME	ACTIVITIES
	MORNING
	AFTERNOON
	EVENING

Word of the Day Diary

Journal: Day 23

DATE: _____ PAGE 3

Nightly Review

TIME	ACTIVITIES
	MORNING
	AFTERNOON
	EVENING

TOTAL HOURS

Writing: _____ Journaling: _____ Research: _____

Ideal Day Planner

TIME	ACTIVITIES
	MORNING
	AFTERNOON
	EVENING

Diary

How would I like to transform my day? How do I feel about my day overall? Did I do enough writing and writing-related tasks?

Journal: Day 24

DATE: _____ PAGE 1

Word of the Day

Conflict Word

Conflict Cluster

Story Idea

NOTES

Journal: Day 24

DATE: _____ PAGE 2

Writing Intentions

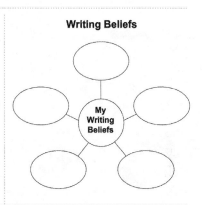

Writing Beliefs

Ideal Day Planner

TIME	ACTIVITIES
	MORNING
	AFTERNOON
	EVENING

Word of the Day Diary

Journal: Day 24

DATE: _____ PAGE 3

Nightly Review

TIME	ACTIVITIES
	MORNING
	AFTERNOON
	EVENING

TOTAL HOURS

Writing: _____   Journaling: _____   Research: _____

Ideal Day Planner

TIME	ACTIVITIES
	MORNING
	AFTERNOON
	EVENING

Diary

How would I like to transform my day? How do I feel about my day overall? Did I do enough writing and writing-related tasks?

Journal: Day 25

DATE: _____ PAGE 1

Word of the Day

(Word of the Day)

Conflict Word

(Conflict Word)

Conflict Cluster

(Conflict Cluster)

Story Idea

NOTES

Journal: Day 25

DATE: _____ PAGE 2

Writing Intentions

My
Writing
Intentions

Writing Beliefs

My
Writing
Beliefs

Ideal Day Planner

TIME	ACTIVITIES
	MORNING
	AFTERNOON
	EVENING

Word of the Day Diary

Journal: Day 25

DATE: _____ PAGE 3

Nightly Review

TIME	ACTIVITIES
	MORNING
	AFTERNOON
	EVENING

Writing: _____ Journaling: _____ Research: _____

TOTAL HOURS

Ideal Day Planner

TIME	ACTIVITIES
	MORNING
	AFTERNOON
	EVENING

Diary

How would I like to transform my day? How do I feel about my day overall? Did I do enough writing and writing-related tasks?

Journal: Day 26

DATE: _____ PAGE 1

Word of the Day

Conflict Word

Conflict Cluster

Story Idea

NOTES

Journal: Day 26

DATE: _____ PAGE 2

Writing Intentions

My Writing Intentions

Writing Beliefs

My Writing Beliefs

Ideal Day Planner

TIME	ACTIVITIES
	MORNING
	AFTERNOON
	EVENING

Word of the Day Diary

Journal: Day 26

DATE: _____ PAGE 3

Ideal Day Planner

TIME	ACTIVITIES
	MORNING
	AFTERNOON
	EVENING

Nightly Review

TIME	ACTIVITIES
	MORNING
	AFTERNOON
	EVENING

TOTAL HOURS

Writing: _____ Journaling: _____ Research: _____

Diary

How would I like to transform my day? How do I feel about my day overall? Did I do enough writing and writing-related tasks?

Journal: Day 27

DATE: _____ PAGE 1

Word of the Day

Conflict Word

Conflict Cluster

Story Idea

NOTES

Journal: Day 27

DATE: _____ PAGE 2

Writing Intentions

My
Writing
Intentions

Writing Beliefs

My
Writing
Beliefs

Ideal Day Planner

TIME	ACTIVITIES
	MORNING
	AFTERNOON
	EVENING

Word of the Day Diary

Journal: Day 27

DATE: _____ PAGE 3

Nightly Review

TIME	ACTIVITIES
	MORNING
	AFTERNOON
	EVENING

TOTAL HOURS

Writing: _____ Journaling: _____ Research: _____

Ideal Day Planner

TIME	ACTIVITIES
	MORNING
	AFTERNOON
	EVENING

Diary

How would I like to transform my day? How do I feel about my day overall? Did I do enough writing and writing-related tasks?

Journal: Day 28

DATE: _____ PAGE 1

Word of the Day

Word of the Day

Conflict Word

Conflict Word

Conflict Cluster

Conflict Cluster

Story Idea

NOTES

Journal: Day 28

DATE: _____ PAGE 2

Writing Intentions

My Writing Intentions

Writing Beliefs

My Writing Beliefs

Ideal Day Planner

TIME	ACTIVITIES
	MORNING
	AFTERNOON
	EVENING

Word of the Day Diary

Journal: Day 28

DATE: _____ PAGE 3

Nightly Review

TIME	ACTIVITIES			
	MORNING			
	AFTERNOON			
	EVENING			

Writing: _____ Journaling: _____ Research: _____

TOTAL HOURS

Ideal Day Planner

TIME	ACTIVITIES			
	MORNING			
	AFTERNOON			
	EVENING			

Diary

How would I like to transform my day? How do I feel about my day overall? Did I do enough writing and writing-related tasks?

Journal: Day 29

DATE: _____ PAGE 1

Word of the Day

Word of the Day

Conflict Word

Conflict Word

Conflict Cluster

Conflict Cluster

Story Idea

NOTES

Journal: Day 29

DATE: _____ PAGE 2

Writing Intentions

My Writing Intentions

Writing Beliefs

My Writing Beliefs

Ideal Day Planner

TIME	ACTIVITIES
	MORNING
	AFTERNOON
	EVENING

Word of the Day Diary

Journal: Day 29

DATE: _____ PAGE 3

Nightly Review

TIME	ACTIVITIES
	MORNING
	AFTERNOON
	EVENING

Writing: _____ Journaling: _____ Research: _____

TOTAL HOURS

Ideal Day Planner

TIME	ACTIVITIES
	MORNING
	AFTERNOON
	EVENING

Diary

How would I like to transform my day? How do I feel about my day overall? Did I do enough writing and writing-related tasks?

Journal: Day 30

DATE: _____ PAGE 1

Word of the Day

Conflict Word

Conflict Cluster

Story Idea

NOTES

Journal: Day 30

DATE: _____ PAGE 2

Writing Intentions

My Writing Intentions

Writing Beliefs

My Writing Beliefs

Ideal Day Planner

TIME	ACTIVITIES
	MORNING
	AFTERNOON
	EVENING

Word of the Day Diary

Journal: Day 30

DATE: _____ PAGE 3

Nightly Review

TIME	ACTIVITIES											
	MORNING											
	AFTERNOON											
	EVENING											

TOTAL HOURS

Writing: _____ Journaling: _____ Research: _____

Ideal Day Planner

TIME	ACTIVITIES											
	MORNING											
	AFTERNOON											
	EVENING											

Diary

How would I like to transform my day? How do I feel about my day overall? Did I do enough writing and writing-related tasks?

O-BOOKS

SPIRITUALITY

O is a symbol of the world, of oneness and unity; this eye represents knowledge and insight. We publish titles on general spirituality and living a spiritual life. We aim to inform and help you on your own journey in this life.
If you have enjoyed this book, why not tell other readers by posting a review on your preferred book site?

Recent bestsellers from O-Books are:

Heart of Tantric Sex
Diana Richardson
Revealing Eastern secrets of deep love and intimacy
to Western couples.
Paperback: 978-1-90381-637-0 ebook: 978-1-84694-637-0

Crystal Prescriptions
The A-Z guide to over 1,200 symptoms and their healing crystals
Judy Hall
The first in the popular series of eight books, this handy little guide is packed as tight as a pill bottle with crystal remedies for ailments.
Paperback: 978-1-90504-740-6 ebook: 978-1-84694-629-5

Shine On
David Ditchfield and J S Jones
What if the aftereffects of a near-death experience were undeniable? What if a person could suddenly produce high-quality paintings of the afterlife, or if they acquired the ability to compose classical symphonies? Meet: David Ditchfield.
Paperback: 978-1-78904-365-5 ebook: 978-1-78904-366-2

The Way of Reiki
The Inner Teachings of Mikao Usui
Frans Stiene
The roadmap for deepening your understanding of the system of Reiki and rediscovering your
True Self.
Paperback: 978-1-78535-665-0 ebook: 978-1-78535-744-2

You Are Not Your Thoughts.
Frances Trussell
The journey to a mindful way of being, for those who want to truly know the power of mindfulness.
Paperback: 978-1-78535-816-6 ebook: 978-1-78535-817-3

The Mysteries of the Twelfth Astrological House
Fallen Angels
Carmen Turner-Schott, MSW, LISW
Everyone wants to know more about the most misunderstood house in astrology — the twelfth astrological house.
Paperback: 978-1-78099-343-0 ebook: 978-1-78099-344-7

WhatsApps from Heaven
Louise Hamlin
An account of a bereavement and the extraordinary
signs — including WhatsApps — that a retired
law lecturer received from her deceased husband.
Paperback: 978-1-78904-947-3 ebook: 978-1-78904-948-0

The Holistic Guide to Your Health
& Wellbeing Today
Oliver Rolfe
A holistic guide to improving your complete health,
both inside and out.
Paperback: 978-1-78535-392-5 ebook: 978-1-78535-393-2

Cool Sex
Diana Richardson and Wendy Doeleman
For deeply satisfying sex, the real secret is to reduce the heat,
to cool down. Discover the empowerment and fulfilment
of sex with loving mindfulness.
Paperback: 978-1-78904-351-8 ebook: 978-1-78904-352-5

Creating Real Happiness A to Z
Stephani Grace
Creating Real Happiness A to Z will help you understand
the truth that you are not your ego
(conditioned self).
Paperback: 978-1-78904-951-0 ebook: 978-1-78904-952-7

A Colourful Dose of Optimism
Jules Standish
It's time for us to look on the bright side, by boosting
our mood and lifting our spirit, both in our interiors,
as well as in our closet.
Paperback: 978-1-78904-927-5 ebook: 978-1-78904-928-2

Readers of ebooks can buy or view any of these bestsellers by
clicking on the live link in the title. Most titles are published
in paperback and as an ebook. Paperbacks are available in
traditional bookshops. Both print and ebook formats are
available online.

Find more titles and sign up to our readers' newsletter at
www.o-books.com

Follow O books on Facebook at **O-books**

For video content, author interviews and more, please subscribe to our YouTube channel:

O-BOOKS Presents

Follow us on social media for book news, promotions and more:

Facebook: O-Books

Instagram: @o_books_mbs

Twitter: @obooks

Tik Tok: @ObooksMBS

www.o-books.com